Left Fields

for David, a guiding light

and

for Ferg (1986 – 2002)
a cat, a gift

CONTENTS

III   **This Is Your Life**

We drove through country we did not know we loved – not rolling or flat, but broken, no recognizable rhythm to it; low hills, hollows full of brush, swamp and bush and fields. Tall elm trees, separate, each plainly showing its shape, doomed but we did not know that either. They were shaped like slightly opened fans, sometimes like harps.

– Alice Munro, *Lives of Girls and Women*

Grow up surrounded by nothing but sustenance,
A monotony of beans, then corn.
Every road cutting through it knows to head out of town.
My home took a step forward, collapsed in on itself.
Why shouldn't it want to lie down in these fields?
Look at the grass growing out shattered windows.
Dirt and small plants curtain the panes.
I open the front door, bare dirt behind it.
I open the front door, dirt scours my name . . .

– Catherine Sasanov, *All the Blood Tethers*

I   Homeland, With Wreckage

Career Day at Diefenbaker High

Here are your options:

You aren't smart enough for
Reach for the Top – strike Rocket Scientist.

You razored your jeans above the thigh
during the school moratorium
on cut-offs – clearly can't follow instructions.

You went dateless to the prom, not knowing
some statements are not
worth making – sign of weak judgement.

You disfigured the hairdresser dummy
in Home Ec. – possible sociopath.

Everything you say can and is
used against you – underdeveloped discretion skills.

Your girlfriend
refused to remember what
you did in the hayloft, you refused
to forget – symptoms of perversion.

The school python is fed three
guinea pigs daily; you can't get
past the sound they make inside
the dark snake – impaired ability to accept basic principles
of nature.

Too melancholy, tall and gawky
for a stewardess, will have to do
something on earth –

Poetry?

St. Paul's Crossing

Not all ghosts are holy.

      I had a brush
with holiness, before
seatbelts, scooting past a dusty farm
      in our tin contraption.
As always, potato salad and summer
      Sundays could kill with
glory.
My green dress, see-through
like Lake Huron, was emerald mist
over my nine-year-old proud knees.
Untethered I sat beside my father.

St. Paul's Crossing. A preacher, hell-bent
for heaven
      nearly sent us there, us, earthly
fodder for his huge
Buick. Dashes to dashes, my mouth

all gravel, glass, gash
of air against
my tongue churned out a new
language of ruin.

My father learned to fly.

Behind their big bandage, my teeth folded
into a steeple.

Broken country

Driving with Daddy   splintered sun
windshield   used my head. Even on pokey roads
Death the hick
snaps his suspenders, yuks it up.
I like
         anything cranberry   I said, then
I forgive him.

Before, they always chanted sleep. Now, stay awake,
must keep her awake. *Scenes of Canada*, crayons.
Lime Lion's Gate Bridge   Polka Dot Prairie
Peggy's Cove beaming out a low black bolt.
Ontario, blue (wake-up royal). Towers, trestles – *hey are you
with us?*

To this day, I'm not ashamed to call
                              myself exalted
patriot. The whole bloody place
kept me awake.

Smile

I lived. Became Jack O'Lantern Girl. Crooked smile better
than none, my mother said, this

being era of sunny disposition, reign of Farrah Fawcett.
Standing on a hay-bale soapbox, I begged
to differ.

Always: *write about your summer vacation.*
Never: *write about an experience of early disfigurement.*

The angels looked out for you, no one
in particular said. Thanks. Will they find me a job that forgives
a jumbled trap, that doesn't require dazzling smile
while pointing to the exit doors?

The girls next door

Two small girls live on the other side of the hedge.
Each morning, they fill their inflatable pool and
finding earwigs, scream *ooooo creepy ooooo gross*!
Once, they debated at length whether
earwigs pinch. Assume they do
you wanted to shout through a long green
tunnel of time. But something made you
remember: there are ways of being
a little girl. Conventions that shouldn't be
tampered with. Poodle barrettes in a world
badly disfigured. Your first house, gift wrapped
in Virginia creeper had a green gloom you loved,
darkly iridescent, but its woody tracks were
rat runways: one looked in your bedroom
window, bared its teeth, and you knew you'd
never be beautiful. Or safe. For now, the creepiness
can be controlled with words, cries of outrage,
that inimitable, prim daintiness small girls hold
graduate degrees in. For now.

Mother teaching her daughter to skate a long time ago

The whole river frozen before you. Forget piano, elocution. You want to marry well, learn elegance on ice. Get up on those elk bone blades and do it. Stop crying, little goose, or I'll give you something to cry *for*. Pay no attention to the animals under your feet; they had terrible lives, barbaric courtships. Urine-soaked stags bugling across miles of cold moss; you'd be living in a harem, foraging along Peace River, instead of having your own house. Get on with it, we don't have all winter. Figures, jumps, spins to be mastered. Imagine the loveliest ribbon uncurling the length of the river, follow it. This is the new calligraphy, my dear, let's make it as graceful as we can. You say you're cold – oh *my*, how we suffer. What am I going to do with you? Sorry shape you're in, and the world's first covered rink opening next month, the coming-out for young ladies everywhere. Competition will be fierce. I hear things. I pay attention. Now I suppose I must bribe and cajole like you're a wee girl again. If you're good, I'll buy you new skates, the latest steel blades. Think of the bright muff I'm stitching for you back home. Your veil folded in the hope chest, covered in shimmering beads. Imagine all those eligible bachelors, long scarves billowing in biting wind. Consider for a moment, if you can, how happy grandchildren would make me. Get up get up *get up*.

Any room we enter

It's black ice, entering
rooms in the middle of things –

They don't make babysitters
like they used to, my husband is saying.

Stop me before I skid
into 1971 – more black ice – the Dragon-Dad

breathing rye driving me
home. It's late. I watched his boys

watch a Leaf score a hat trick, enormous
in his warehouse of pads. The Zamboni

made everyone strange, even the dragon
who never saw the game. Enough snow

to fishtail, he's never seen the concession
so thick. His Brylcream gleams, he hands

me five bucks, thumb pressing
the side of my knee – that's how they made

babysitters, then. We came with second-degree
burns of shame. Show me any room we enter

surefooted, from scratch.

Crowning glory

Sky's apricot scarf floats down
over the lake, day
is dethroned. Toronto's lights are tiaras
the dark water dances back.

Under lamps on poles, the carnival
breathes its deepest, its
Getcher little doggie here
best. Ostrich marionettes are
learning to walk. There are foot-
long hot dogs, pretzels baked into knots.
The Bulova clock towers, a white plate
with worried parent hands.
Drifters (men with bandannas, greased arms we were
warned away from) tighten bolts
on rides that pitch people into
                    each other's laps.

Crickets scritched along the edges.

On this night, someone was named
Miss CNE 1973,
and someone was not: a girl all curves
one farm over from me (I was her
curling-iron caddy, number one friend).

It was a long day in Beauty Queen Land.

Under a dome holding a vast, refrigerated swan
sculpted from butter a blonde in sequins
announced *the end to a glorious day*
for all eighty contestants.

                    Flashbulbs.
                    Roses.
The winners wept, swarmed
by loss.

My best friend bent over Lake Ontario,
dropped mascara tears (little grey doves)
into its silver. Tore off her wrist corsage, flung it
at the big dipper's handle and
fired me as her manager.
                    Sky, for a moment
held the cinnamon musk
of carnations, the night's crowning glory.

Shania: a Canadian tale

There was once a girl named Eileen. She laid a rose
on her mother's grave. Needless to say, she was
very sad. She sang stupid songs, danced dumb dances
at the Huntsville resort to buy groceries. She changed
her name to Shania, Ojibwa for: *I'm on my way.* And
she was.

There was once a girl named Nobody. She had no career.
She was very sad. One day, Nobody gazed in her glass, noted
a striking likeness to the star, Shania Twain. Why hadn't
the Career Counsellor explained the art of resemblance? Nobody
could carry a tune. And she did. Across Canada.

There is a poet. She lives in faraway woods where
no stars ever stop. She is very sad. Her sole
consolations: twenty-twenty vision and close reading skills.
She spies a sign:
Shania Twin, One Night Only! She can't believe
her eyes: country diva, singer of *Whose Bed Have Your Boots Been
Under?* at her doorstep.

Our backwoods poet dons her satin shirt, grabs her pen, hoofs it
to her local arena, only to find some cheap impersonator.
She is very chastened. She writes a poem.

Adventures in moving

Whoever didn't drive counted
the overturned U-hauls
since Edmonton, the lives
ditched in loosestrife.
       Once a stuffed clown
grasped Yellowhead Highway's yellow
line for dear life.
Thistles grew through lawn
chairs' cross-hatched seats. There were
many books.
We said we were pulling
over to stretch, not amble through
someone's dead library
       (one book was called
       Mental Drills in Rapid Calculation).
Many had the same Visionware
pots as ours.

The trailers said "Adventures in Moving"
upside down, any way an alphabet
shakes into ruin.

That morning
we bargained over what must be left
to magpies: my old flamingo dresser,
drawers stacked beside
a "take me" sign – isn't that what
       moves are, grim
generosities?

Last thing we need:
tobacco-wadding prairie prophet
holding court beside his gas pump
in the vast, slithering heat:
> *Trouble with young people today is,*
> *they don't know how to*
> *distribute the load. See it all*
> *the time: pathetic, pathetic.*

                So. We were part of
a great pathos, a rapid calculation
moving east. World
baked and strewn with
a single ambition: to remain
right-side up.
We stopped counting
                somewhere near Oxdrift.

What we learned on the highway near St. John's

That bakeapples are not baked, nor apples.
Two boys waving jars above their heads. In grand sweeping arcs.
We thought "accident" but

why the jars? We pulled our rampant-with-rust American car over.
No sign of blood.
No Camaro slicing the grizzled bush. The boys were freckled, as
boys in summer are. Denim torn at the knees.
                          We opened our windows.

The jars were filled with tiny, plush globes, the smallest of
pumpkins. *Bakeapples*, they said. *Best served over vanilla
ice-cream. Only grow on the island.*
They spoke of muskeg and thorns, hours of hunting.

We bought all four, pleased what we thought
an accident was a new way of knowing
apples. Driving away, we looked back at the boys,
                          waving, their hands empty.

Answering my American friends

What providence do I live in? I wish.
You must be thinking of province.
Yes, there's only one road. Townships so small
they don't show up on dental x-rays.
That's why I talk funny. Yes, we're still deciding how to exist.
To do this, we send our leaders to a nice resort, call it Referendum,
Royal Commission, Accord.
The rest of us watch on TVs in panelled, antlered bars,
hear it radioed in bush camps,
the sound of one land snapping. We never quite break.
We spend much time fixing on a higher plane, trying to transcend
our bodies (what is a body, but one big opportunity?).
Occasionally, a pretender arises. He'll be beaten down by satire.
We're funny as hell.
Our women dream of men without winches.
I'm flattered you find me exotic. Yes, many of us have dark roots.

Gutter and gloves

1.

Anka

1956. I'm not just another lonely
blue boy. Just a hundred bucks, Pop – I'll sing
of Diana the babysitter (she's so old) in New York, sell them
everything, you'll see. I'll make Vegas, break the Iron
Curtain – that blowhard Feld who said *take a hike, kid*
backstage in Ottawa – some day he'll *beg*
to manage me. I'll have my own hockey team – leave
the gutter behind – so long, sewer workers who threw coins
as I crooned. My eyes: dames can't resist
those dark orbs. I'll date Annette Funicello, if I
want, write her a song, don't laugh, Pop.

2.

Gould

My hands. My hands are threads. Stop staring,
they'll disappear. Summer's worst, kill
that infernal cold-air machine. My gloves
need gloves, my fingers a warm bath. Lucky I brought my kettle
and yesterday was shock-therapy. These glaring white keys
give me knuckle-rash. Sand them down, these terrible ivory slabs,
take a good set of steak knives, carve them up and for God's sake,
don't hound me again
about silly scales, I hear Bach
laughing from here.

To go back

To discover those small rolling townships ironed into a place
with a big flat name. To find Glenelg, only
palindrome you know

gone. To see the few farmers left fumble across their land,
their fingers a final compass. To bet someone told them don't
take it personal.

To smell mould on the corduroy swatches in your 4-H book.
To feel severely chipped away at. To hear bat wings
hammer through the homestead, over white, parental heads.
To wonder how can they
                              live like this.

To book a hotel nearby. To have a bottle of piss fired at your door
in the night. To realise this passes
for drive-by shooting in this new amalgamated world.

To be shot. To witness the sun sag upward. To hope
all the dark flying things got lost. To listen while your mother says
if she doesn't eat this minute she'll fall

into a coma. To sense a palindromic itch come over you.
To need air. To cruise a decrepit flea market, snag a thesaurus.
To read regress means loss of ground. To think

surprise, surprise. To go back. To talk to doomed elms
that sometimes looked like harps. To find your father
                              kind to you, saddest
thing of all.

More bridge shots

O you've   been there   done that   got the t-shirt
worldly one   loner   daughter-of-farmwife
sole matinee-watcher – *The Bridges of Madison County.*
(The projectionist regrets crashed air conditioner – popcorn-on-
house hardly the solace you'd hoped). Meltdown, you
               enter the screen's flicker-spell –

peppery road   boot-camp corn   farmwife's few days
alone   sexy drifter with camera   his shots
through screen doors pickups   icebox slowly
slowly open-
          ing

(Why do farmers grow surly?) Must it always
come to longing? Dust? More bridge shots   lumbering, canopied,
                    old from every conceivable
angle (easy, falling
for artisan of the eye). There's hope for you yet   you still weep
when the story says – her hand   her hand on the truck door
        rain, the irrevocable left turn. His   leaving (signal).

"We're not meant to pity the farmwife," your sage colleague
would later expound – "choosing not to choose
signifies choice" (o you
           hater of
              genius). That's not
how it happened, what do lecturers know of
the land   *your* fields –

brittle montage   mauve-washed   further light,
funnelling: the lane   dust-filmed   begging your
        mother-the-farmwife
to leave   take you   your small, small
voice in the wood house riddled at both ends, like a
covered bridge.

O sage colleague, we *are* meant to pity   we are.

Brave

is a word you must grow
into, wait while it sheds
its patronising skin. *Be brave*, taller people
said in waiting rooms.

Brave

needs to season like wine your mother made
from dandelions between chores meant for a man
twice her size. No wonder she made her own
yellow medicine, asterisks of summer to soothe backaches.

Not so dear as store-bought.

She is eighty-three now, shorter
than you. With her in the examination room
your skull fills with the lilacs
she heaped over your birthdays
to cover the absence of gifts.

The doctor says *curvature of the spine*.

A life of farming, she says.

You want to say it's the way any mauve branch would
bend into May. You want to say it's only the dance of the brave,
tenacious spring. Bones at a glance
tell so little. You've been watching her for years, only
now see her, a brave woman with lilacs
picking her way along the white, gnarled path,
the vertebrae of love.

II   **Can Anything Save a Daughter?**

The orphan collector

First its hoof pushed into the world, pointing –
faithful compass – yes, *there* is where
I want to go. Then birth's bilge, broken
and red on the straw, outgrown balloon. Shift
to the mother's tongue, nose
deciding whether she wants it or
it tastes smells too much like the world, not
enough like her. So lowering
her head, butts it clear

into weather. This is where I came in, the orphan collector.

The lamb made the most adorable errors,
mistook the soft flesh on the back of my leg
for a breast. *I'm better than your mean mother*
I'd blurt, holding its milk bottle or pulling it
in my red wagon, its long, droopy ears
rumbling over potholes.
Raised in the church I'd founded on the doctrine
that nature's barbarism could be overcome
the lamb grew smaller, was soon
the size of an infant's sweater. Then still.

*God already decided all this, it has nothing
to do with you*, the farmers' wives said.

The air bristled with heretics, in those days.

The great era of aerial photography

Barn roofs
were photogenic, then.
Pilots with cameras shot our farm, tendered
its image, seen from above. We could never
not buy (the flying eyes had time-
purchase plans for people
like us).
      This wasn't sky stalking, this
was magic. Spellbound, we couldn't get over
the quaint, scattered cartons
called home. String of lane, poplars stunned
in a grey breeze. The ranch reborn, vaguely
               scientific.
Every few years, another plane
portrait and though we'd several already, thanks,
we could never be sure something
hadn't moved. So we'd add the new views
to our air album.
In them, we never found
even a flicker of ourselves, pail bearers passing
from shed to shed (one blemish we
suspected the dog). *You're down there
somewhere*, the hawkers all said, crop-
dusting their smiles
while my mother penned the latest
series of post-dated cheques.

The Ken Madsen path to town

Is any of this free will?
Thick skulls with their dinosaur attitudes.
                                        –Barry Dempster

Comfort's a thespian, a tricky headline
never quite herself. *There have been no cougar sightings*
for eighteen months – can you really feel
cosy about that? To reach town, you must
walk a path through woods and think
as you do, of your all-time-top-ten poems
it *will* cross your mind:
cougar, cougar, burning bright
in the lodgepoles of the night –
Is any of this free will?

To reach town, you must pass the grave
of John and Margaret Straw, observe
because you can, how their smooth
black stone with its mild, pleasing-to-
the-eye arch resembles a mountain worn
way down. This is what getting to town
costs. The spell of similitude, is this
solace? Better than cougars? You wish
you'd known the Straws. And the other headstones?
Thick skulls with their dinosaur attitudes.

Jogging

Gravel road. Night. She runs
past a barn that's down
on one knee. New shadows.
        Coyotes.
Dogs have been disappearing. Story is
coyotes won't
bother if
you're not one
of them. This must be the sequel. Jagged
little hoots near
her heels. Twenty pounds all
she wants to lose.

She runs. Is this Darwin's revenge set loose
on Nova Scotia's back roads, this wild
wolfish thing tracking her whimpery
puppy heart?

        Ahead: distant light: home:
mint tea, freesias in crockery. Home: where she'll laugh at
silly old her
throw the dead bolt
mail order a Stairmaster.

Mirrors in Mexico

Framed like rococo cottages with little doorways you can
enter or not. If you don't, you still

have the cottage, its pink hearts, scalloped eaves.
No stalker wolf. Only your face

as folk art. Where you come from, mirrors
can do math, eat you alive, occupy whole skyscrapers, malls.

You are buying your lemons and Tampax and
there you are

buying your Tampax and lemons. No way around
the silver, snarling air.

The Guess Who **play North Bay – One Night Only**

Wall mounted, Big Mouth Billy Bass
dances and sings to eighties rock.
Puts his whole soul and fin
into it. I hear him in a rambly Nipissing bar, on my way
to 'Rockettes' (door with skirt silhouette
next to 'Rockers').

In the tiny bathroom, three women play
air guitar, sing:
>   *American woman, get away from me-hee,*
>   *American woman, mama, let me be-hee.*
Their big-haired, tequila joy
surrounds me: I *must* party with them,
hear *The Guess Who.*
I'm here to read poetry.
Well, read it, they say. *Right here*
right now. In the john. They are not
small women. The redhead keeps wailing
on guitar, locking her jaw to one
side then the other.
>   Maybe this is how
poetry *should* happen, I muse, backed into
the Kotex machine. Dispensed
through a haze of air
guitar riffs, funny notions
of social power. Bad-girl-locker-room stuff.

Homesickness.

And notwithstanding lakes
I still miss like lovers, the north goes on
in the limo's long sweep
towing national rock stars through rock, comes out

the other side, the mouths
of singing fish
macho party-girls
the cry for poetry *right here right now*

the way each day is lived like the last
gig you'll ever get.

What the poem wants

– a dog a nice house a ticket
with a blank return date, a long
night's sleep after shooting
pool past last call. The poem
wants it all.
      The poem wants to wear
its habit with its pink polyester
pant suit. Arm-wrestled then tucked in,
told a story. The poem wants
to beat the crap out of you then
make love. The poem wants to be alone,
a puritan watching an orgy through
a crack in the alphabet.
      The poem
wants to be wanton, to know
when to hold up, when
to fold up, to be coddled then pushed
into a cold bottomless, very clear
lake after which
it understands at last
what it really wants:

the poem wants you
to watch while
it drowns.

Duke

"That's my last Duchess painted on the wall,
Looking as if she were alive."

– Robert Browning

Chill, he'd say, *chill*. It had become my Duke's mantra.
Call to Zen?
A kind of 'it's alright, mama?'
                                        Not a chance.
He'd snarl it like you'd hurl it at a rabid fox you were angling
to corner then snag in a jumbo net, the kind you've viewed
on the wildlife channel. Or
seen through a more
                                        domestic gaze, he'd say it like you'd tell
a dog *heel*.

If you didn't know Duke, you'd guess him
some harmless old biker, the kind who rents *Easy Rider*
and eats brownies once a week.

It's here somewhere, man, the cautionary tale, here at the end
of me, I'm the mutt, the little woman. The stuffed heron
on the sill, looking as if
                                        I'm alive.

Dead people's clothes

In Annapolis Royal, we stepped on a soldier
dead two hundred years: sorry:
what else could we say? Then we had drinks.

A Full Professor I know doesn't want his wife
wearing dead people's clothes. This is based
on unsound logic (his wife

isn't dead). In the apple capital, Berwick
Frenchy's (over the feed store) we fill our baskets
with glorious rags, school clothes

silver dinner dress, anorak. What goes around.
These are stories of human exertion, sweat
stains under white t-shirt arms. Labour, a whole

wall of maternity togs. Weighty ambition, epic
shoulder pads. Seduction, tiny crotchless things
in the far bin. Brooks Brothers suit (my husband

says in case there's a funeral). The place smells
like New England, old L.L. Bean. I wear
someone's Nantucket sundress, good for me. We are

what the ships drag in, what we unearth, warp
and woof, here's a dog's sweater, they've thought of
everything (warm loyalist pets). It's all here:

.

the fields we've left, the skins we've shed,
the lives we've led. Barn shirts. A doll with
pathos for a face. Armour in case

there's a war. The Blossom Festival was
last weekend; aside from that, things remain
quiet, the cashier says, sorting a tray of buttons.

Aside from the occasional squabble over high
end linen, the odd *this is to die for*
cried out in pure wool ecstasy, rebirth.

Shooting the little bear

I had a date with Heraclitus.
There was a lot of flux. Call me Harry, he said, and
from a distance, he looked sexy and tough,
like Callahan in the Dirty Harry pictures. But when
I got close, he said, Call me Doctor, for God's sake, show
some respect for a great philosopher; soon he was on
to something else. It was all blur, maybe the casino-girl
costume, that night...(?) I'm telling you this to make it stop. But
damn it, he made me laugh, so I went with him again, carnival, this
time. I couldn't shoot the little bear, so he
made me cry. I shot the little bear, that was worse. Of course
we made up, such an endless array of
positions. Our bodies are landscapes we never
recover from, he explained in a sage outburst followed by:
I know I called you boring and
insulted your earrings, but that was yesterday.
Will you see me again?
He looked small, fuzzy and vulnerable
in the receding light, so I said, possibly, ask me
again tomorrow.
So we're on again, off again, Harry and I, and like
everything else, it does
and it doesn't.

Dreams: two families at the end of civilisation

i)
Diarists, record keepers, taxidermists, home movie makers,
precise thinkers, barometer-trackers, bibliophilic
pack rats. No calendar thrown away ever. Never
know when you might need to know how often April Fool's
fell on Monday. And don't come home all sloppy-minded
saying you saw a butterfly: you saw *lepidoptera*, was it
mourning cloak, tiger swallowtail, or what? Write it down
so you'll remember next time. On Judgement Day
those without accounts, they'll be the ones caught with
their pants down.

ii)
The mother mixing a cake at the counter. School over,
the kid winding down the lane into the sugar-aired kitchen.
Hello, the mother says, cheerfully. What's your name again?
Oh dear, did I remember eggs? Yes, it's a little hot for baking
but I wasn't going to let your birthday pass without a cake.
It's *not* your birthday? Well, we'll have a nice cake anyway,
la la la. Windows open, every imaginable thing that flies
in neon or lollipop shades
is in there, swooping and dipping and double-flipping over
the mixing bowl. The smiling mother points: an iridescent
whatchamathinger, it hovers. More kids pour into the kitchen,
dodging wings, no one can say what day it is, they only know
it's no one's birthday. More tots: twins, triplets, diaper wearers.
Everyone wants to lick the beaters, she'll find a way, she's
the mother. She'll make everything come up bonbons, whatever
day this is, it's the happiest day of their lives.

Weapon of mouse destruction

After a quarter century of Sunday
phone calls home, I should know
there are no innocent questions. Weather
leads to death, terminal skids
off glass roads. But pets,
pets are always a safe topic
aren't they? How's the cat?
He caught a mouse, my mother says,
juggled it alive so she
finished it off with her cane.

That was two Sundays ago.
I'm still sickened by the image:
old woman's walking stick bludgeons
little mouse face. The relish
in her voice. I will never
get over my mother. Never be allowed

old-lady clichés, the luxury
to imagine a sweet senior bearing
down on her cane. Never be freed from
her kitchen, land of the hunted.

Moose whistles

Tomorrow I'll drive far
north alone. Today
my father brings home moose whistles
from Canadian Tire.

His fingers, gnawed by binder twine
unpeel the sticky whistle-backs. He bends
over my blue Plymouth, positioning
them.
      The neighbours watch,
Elmer not asking
how hollow bullets beside headlights
could save me. Selma (who writes poetry)
not venturing we are all
blindfolded moths limping along our
trajectories of pathos: young Murray not
mumbling how
dark it gets, up there. Even the old man
whose *Scientific American* came
to us by mistake refrains from
insisting on proof:
      can two squeals in the night
keep boreal beasts away? Can anything
save a daughter?

On rereading Flannery O'Connor's "Good Country People"

Opening the book, it all happens again:

A bible salesman steals a good
country girl's wooden leg. She only
wanted love up there in the barn.
Nothing like that ever happened
to me; the chicken-loading boys
hooted only once, no matter how many
reasons to wear my cutoffs
past their truck stacked with
soup-bound panic, crates
they threw about handily for
they were brawny, the boxes light
with open spaces, finely spun
maple bars someone stood turning
on a lathe while imagining a love
free from tricks. I couldn't
pay someone to take
something from me, then.
                    The girl in the story
was a tough Ph.D. with two names:
one homely, one pretty.
The bible bag held
only sex toys. I know how she feels. By now
I'm hardly illiterate myself, having
thought deeply and gazed
into the world's ugly chops. Watch out –

they'll take your beautiful one
every time, shut your wings down then
laugh about it. What? You
like my hair? Well, gosh, I'm sure it must've
bits of hay sticking to it. Yes, you can
touch it, go ahead.

A brief history of bison

There's a dead bison at the end
of my driveway
         (startling, since bison were
last seen herded over
cliffs two centuries ago) its carcass so bulky,
immense, I can hardly see the winterised
trailer across the street.

A landscape company left the bison
with these words:
Shovel liberally on gardens, under shrubs,
trees, any place without
a history. Repeat if needed.

Around me, scrapes and heaves of spades. Seems everyone
had a bison dropped off.

Happy Earth Day, the neighbour says, bits of bison
on his denim knees. *Happy happy* echoes from
driveway to driveway.

That's what I like about
this place, everyone digs in. By sunset, all the bison
are gone.
         What a town –
blink and you   won't   miss a thing.

The Horse Whisperer

Horses have it worse
after accidents, if
the movies have it right.
Humans can function
in all sorts of marred
conditions but horses
must be flawless; this belief
comes from too much
mythology. Movie: hurt
horse pulled to Montana,
booked with an expensive
faith healer who's a ringer
for Robert Redford. The horse
won't trust anyone until
she's *certain* it's
Robert Redford, so many men
look like him. It takes time,
this trust in blonde, rugged guys
with fancy rope work. But there's
something about him, the jaded
but attractive female horse-owner
sees it too. Something to do
with how light hits worn denim,
the porch slants west and
each planet, if she squints
after enough Mexican beer,
resembles a tiny cure, fizzing
and popping, then gone.

This can't possibly be my life

To prove I'm not
          stranded, I roll my sleeping
bag into a tidy oversized cigar
each morning. Any minute, I could vanish
in smoke, everything's that
provisional. Like camp. All I leave
behind: one dying cat, an old wizard I love more
than most people.

I wash, blow-dry my coat.
I strike out, raging
over the brief lives
of animals, the siege
beneath Wizard's fur. I blame
those snoozing in my English class for
this and for
the demise of any and all grammars
of compassion. For institutional ennui.
I tramp the halls hard in my boots, pray I'm hurting the tiles,
the light fading at last.

Back at camp, drugged puss, having grown
smaller, warms another spot of time on the bare mattress.
"You won't believe the daydream I had," I tell her:
"I was a truth-dispenser, the awake ones
were dropping coins
in my mouth like
          a pop machine. As each coin hit
the pit of me, it said, in its tinny
coin voice: *drink this –*
this is your life, this is what it costs."

III   This Is Your Life

The new stories

Morning's a girl in a gored skirt, playing accordion. Who wouldn't
    want her lilting breeze fanning your face, her fingers on
    those adorable buttons?

Make no mistake. The girl knows she's not
    fashionable. No one speaks of accordionists, now, or
    one-eyed ploughs. No one spins yarns. The new stories are
    set in airports, are blunt, without

punch lines. *They made me unzip my fly. We had to remove*
    our shoes. They kept my best lipstick. They didn't like
    the way my watch looked at them. They move along with
    little awe. The morning wears saddle shoes, taps them

to her bright, heaving pleats. The skirt has poodles. This isn't
    an era for poodles though she's heard they're
    highly intelligent. That's why this

isn't. There's a war. A stiff wind beats in from the east, blasts
    morning's skirt skyward (no one thinks of Marilyn
    Monroe).

Our morning girl has been hiding
    painfully thin legs, hoping to smuggle
    herself into afternoon. She isn't anyone in particular,
    just some

flake from left field, no one you know. She shows up
    here every day, her song
                    broken and brief.

Missing

one of those nights the chest aches with emptiness
which part of me is missing?
　　　　　　　　　 – b.p. nichol, "late night summer poem"

One of those days the sternum sinks lower than a film
by Lars Von Trier, patio drapes best kept
closed. Morning is ambitious – one ray
in the door, the things I love will
crumble to dust. As for lilacs, I've waited too long,
see them only as sacrificial symbol – not sweet
recompense. It's always Judgement Day somewhere;
you've seen those rows of clocks over check-in desks
near the *Sightseers' Fact Sheets.* The only true map
leads to sleep, *one of those nights the chest aches with emptiness*

and the dream's a rerun, horror; Ken the Guidance Counsellor.
I've circled the best answer for each of the following. Ken says
I'm not the chandelier's brightest bulb. In the midst of
trying to improve, I wake up older, at the sea's edge
which strikes me as unduly harsh punishment. Someone's always
eating the last supper, asking for an extra scoop
of dessert. O I wish I'd not frittered away the century
on bibliographies and Eagles songs (*desperado, why don't you*
come to your senses?). This is the common
sense revolution. If it's broke, fix it. Ask, prodigal,
which part of me is missing?

Markings

Sometimes I wish the land had markings
clear as *Pilgrim's Progress.* When you reach
The Slough of Despond, you know
where you are. There's a sign
not far from here, Marshy Hope, but no place
to go with it. There's an island
where lives, much of the world believes, an orphan
with red hair. She's never been home.
There's a regal shore where fishermen dance,
women gather moss in utter contentment. No one
has ever found it.
                    Look at the Vikings.
They heard about a land where you could hump and
eat grapes all day, sailed for it. Reaching
the Great Northern Peninsula, they beat their fists
against the permafrost, wept bitterly.
The road to Cape Breton is filled with giant
buslike things called *Airstream, Endeavour,*
Dutch Star. Not so different from Viking Ships.
The travellers inside have tanned arms, plastic cards.
No idea how lost they are.

The wrecker

He's come down from the mountain
for our last-legs car but
                    doesn't discuss it, leans
into it, redplaid shirt shouldering rust off
the driver's door. Unshaven, showing a burly
disdain for town. Finally, he speaks:

You seen all that bush along the Trans-Canada, all those trees?

                    They're not fuckin' real.

We're lost until he says loggers
left a wall of green. Behind it, carnage. He's come down to say
we've been tricked all this time, driving our ruin
through a stage set, what we thought
wilderness.

He laughs, lights a smoke. He's shown us
what's really going on. We'll take
                    anything for the beater now.

Bog

In dreams, everyone's doing normal things
but naked, covered in mud:
finance seminars given, trucks driven,
politician-words whacked home
with mega-mud gestures. No one seems to mind the soiled carpets,
we're all mired

in our lives, I guess, the calf-roped rooms
of our hearts. It's a living. I'm a Woman Mud Wrestler
(all those student loans), snarling at the mucky-mucks
in the ring (nice college girls like me, making do

in a tough job market). We claw and spit, our boss says folks
pay good money to see she-wolf combat (I don't mind
telling you, it's staged).

After another day in the late-capitalist boglands, the girls and I
like to go for a pint. "Mud in your eye," we'll say, raising a glass
to our art, each other's health. After a few, we'll confess we're
through, next gig *really* our last. Days off, we listen to Muddy
Waters, shower and shower, try to awake, cleansed.

Current

the sweet smell of the water – and finally, the sense of being carried
by a current I could not name or change.
— Marie Howe, "The Dream"

You were trained to count your blessings.
When Santa brings one sock, say "thanks
for stopping by." You get the picture – or half of it, at least.
Aspire to be wizard's aid, not
The Wizard Himself. Some things aren't for us to know.
This way, you'll never be treated for hubris. Learn to live
by halves. That way, you won't need a halfway house.
This is the gospel of Saugeen Flats, this lore
those who swallow swallow whole. And that water
glass question, the answer's half empty. Don't confuse
God's irrigation plan with *the sweet smell of the water*
– and finally, the sense of being carried

down the devil's waterslide into a whirlpool of pride. Remember,
wet or dry, you come from a minor tributary of a small river
running into a tertiary lake no one picnics beside. Certainly not
lovers. So don't beget fancy ideas or if you must, keep them secret.
Deny any sex though if forced to confess, say you closed
your eyes and thought of the queen, say everything can be better.
God didn't lay down those waterways for your personal gain.
Should you commit the ultimate putting-on of airs, writing, strike
all the 'I's'. Should any 'I' survive, say, on Judgment Day, it
happened *by a current I could not name or change.*

Summer house, Southampton, 1939

The kitchen faced the shore, the first beach
my mother, the hired girl,
had ever seen. Behind the screen door
she fell hard for the *whoosh* and *slosh*
of lake, love

at first sound. Soon, she could hear faraway
small things: sand sliding down a toddler's shovel,
distant dogs *ruck rucking* along the edge, water
fights, lovers shouting: *now, stop!*
                    Seen through screen, the world
arranged itself in bright, dancing dots. Heaven through a veil
as she peeled potatoes, cucumbers,
all those skins making her sigh (my mother always
sighed so well). They liked their cucumber salad
sliced real thin. Sweets even in the heat: raisin pie,
hand-turned ice cream. Meringue.

She learned a way of skimming down
while looking out through the screen, never once
cutting herself.
                    Saturdays she laid down
her paring knife, went
outside, at last. Water licking her ankles
was enough, toes simmering in sand
                    more than enough.

There was a carousel, pipey little song.
Later, lanterns, shore spurting bonfires. Those days
before I floated in her
she filled her pockets with shells (to admire
next week), nearly forgot
she was the peeling girl who couldn't swim.

Water lilies

Near morning, but still deep dream
country: lidded land where
we flutter, membranes with
hummingbird hearts, we are

       travelling together, my mother and I.
We've always wanted to see Paris,
Monet's water lilies. It is
springtime (of course), wisteria
waiting to pull on her long, yellow gloves until
our number comes up.

(For years, we'd woven this trip
from words and Lotto 649.)

We are on the Paris subway. *Le Métro*.
I am grabbing the pole
leaning back spinning the way girls
in movies do without
dizziness. I am wearing
something bright, my mother is
laughing in English.
       The names of stops
are jewels. We choose 'Abbesses' because
we love the word and this
is our trip.

I take my mother's arm, the same arm
I took at 'Jane' or 'Castle Frank'.

Ascending
into art-deco garden   'Abbesses'
slips an exquisite
trellis shawl around us. We say
*isn't it something, the way everything
is art here?*

Then – a slowing
of eye movement? – we remember
we forgot our coats on *Le Métro*.
I shout downstairs into
the cavern, *Vite! Vite!* dreaming this
means *Stop! Stop!*

My mother is sure there's something
important in her pocket (but all
she keeps there
are diaphanous scarves from Five-To-A-Dollar).
The coats came
from Value Village.

The train's gone, swallowed by some
faraway trumpet. What was this
stop called again, something quick?
My eyes stop. I am thinking this is just how
we would travel if

we travelled: two butterflies leaving behind
the names of things. Old film footage, people
hurrying along in little halts faster than
they would alive. Two women
looking for lilies and how
they throw long ropes down
into their own histories.

Daughter
swimming up through sleep
awakening to clock
radio, Nova Scotia sleet flinging itself
against the window, alone.

Post

Even asleep, I get mail – thin mean snail letters, snarky slips
(my inner pretender
never rests). "We don't want someone who can 'carry a tune'"
– one letter quoted me in an ugly way – "we want *music*."
(So I called myself qualified for first soprano, what's so depraved
about that? How did they know
it wasn't me, belting out *Unchained Melody*? The world is filled
with snitches.)

        I awake to winter drip, another job in rodeo city
gone. I recall yesterday's door-to-door fundraiser for Benefit
of the Doubt. She wore blue velvet gloves, I gave her my last
five dollars.

Mailmares are worst in winter – cold clobbery
of no's, positions I didn't even
apply for – Moron-In-Residence, Part-time Heartbreaker.
                Busker, sing me
                   a song of dark ambition
before dawn soup-lines the east. Before the big, whistley postman
lugs his regrets
            into the light.

You have mail, Charlotte Brontë

Always mail-time somewhere, sisters in wait-and-fetch.
Good things come in small packets, they say (lowers
our expectations). Somewhere aslant a willow, year anything,
someone tears into test results; the air where
child support should be: missing in action list; boredom of more
bills of goods.

You can't tell me you don't hope
for something big. Don't claim, after dabbing your eyes with lace,
you haven't cursed the carrier of bad/no news. I can hear
your skirts swish (all twelve of them, fending off damp), feel
your ruined tooth throb once more, quake while
your fingers open Robert Southey's dank missive:

> *My dear Miss Brontë, you will never be a poet.*

This cold spring morning, the plastic lid thunks, my own writing
returns in jet-lagged manila. The wretched orphan
is back. It has been drizzling since 1836.

I write:

> *Dear Charlotte:*
> *Pay no attention to the Poet Laureate. Your gifts remain*
> *boundless.*
> *P.S. I'm sure you know cloves*
> *if you can procure them, may numb the pain in your jaw.*

I'll post these words to the grim earth. All we can do: huddle
by our fires, pick up our pens.

Six smaller landscapes, after A.M. Klein's "Portrait Of The Poet As Landscape"

No one understood missing
persons more. Or shadows. The aquatic nature
of landscape. The Poet
— A.M. Klein

1.
No reading lamps on tonight, everyone gone
to see *Titanic*. To cry blockbuster tears, they think it's all
about drowning.

In a glass case in Halifax airport, a replica
death list from the Titanic. Not everyone
could be accounted for: boiler men, stowaways, poets.

Lost. Like in the poem.

2.
Bodies. Tear-shaped pools in good neighbourhoods. Therapists
just up the street. Nothing worked. Wear Tommy Hilfiger shirts,
get dismissed as harmless. One day, words sprouted out
his ears and bloomed; no one paid any attention.

3.
Flowers became him, gave him colour. He opened
a can of dog food, worked his way around, *rimp, rimp*, the dog
came running.

In other cities, others had sprouted, too, screamed in cafés.

4.
What was going on? He was getting email for
someone else, his wife staying later and
later at work.

He didn't look like himself. Leaves began to
web the corners of the pool like those old gold photo corners
but he was too distracted to take the long pole and
fish them out.

5.
Or not to be. Fishing was not the thing. He would never be
one of them, his neighbours with *gone fishing* bumper stickers.
Baseball caps.

The rest was insomnia.

6.
He took up gardening. Not there, in those

straightjacket streets, but in a place no one
would find. Off the map. Being missing not
so bad. He took up singing,
astronomy, too.

Invented his own songs. So much to be said

for perspective. For seeing closer from
far away.

And the sky?

this he would like to write down in a book! And

all of it. Most days now

                        felt incandescent.

Love poem disguised as carpentry

He worshipped a poet, assembled her desk, spent
three days, instructions in eight languages none of which
English. He mustered empires of bolts, braces, screws, crosspieces
into legs, a smooth surface fit
for a pen-wielding prima donna.

The desk carried the scent of his devotion,
the damasked rose he left in its top drawer.
He pulled out her chair like he did when they dined
at a fine restaurant or even
a not-so-fine one. She was seated,
said *silence please*, wrote a poem, spent a day
hanging her pretty wallpaper
down the page. Will she praise carpentry next time they ask
from whence comes her art?

The icicle hunter

(January 1, 2001)

You read the outdoor thermometer – *good day, zero.*
I like places where nothing
is something. Weather, like art,
raises our standards.

Resolution for new year: leave behind chemicals
in tap water. Wash hair in rain – a more pure
link to weather.

Luckily, this is a month of fierce, clear javelins
arrowing down from the eaves. You go hunting,
return with a crystal sword you melt
in the white bucket. For me. My hair.

Standing in your parka, holding that perfect, long streak of glass,
I knew you weren't simply *saying*
you loved me.

My hunter returns, bearing
the iciest gift; it's a grand zero day, the world all
snowy rise, homecoming, a scene
from Brueghel's *Hunters in the Snow.*

Warm ice falls through my scalp. Kneading
my shampoo blizzard, I know
someone on skates circles a cold lake beyond my life, loops and
leaps in the best part of art.

Beside herself

She loves the scene in *Big*
where Tom Hanks, disguised as an adult, leaps on the jumbo piano
and plays *Chopsticks* with his feet. It's contagious. His corporate
boss really a grownup
jumps on board, double the fun.

She's beside herself. How she wishes *her* boss might be tempted to
a game of darts, the moon the board. Or a member of senior
administration join her long enough to pluck a duet on a giant
banjo, she swinging on her string, he on his, both braying with
mirth.

She wishes everything larger. She longs to say we're innocents
who happen to be
big-boned. But she knows we're, in fact, small-boned and growing
smaller.

She shuts her eyes, the sneakers in her mind carry her to the edge
of the carnival. It works every time. She prays for a machine to
take her back. When
she opens her eyes, she's still in her office. The corporation,
no one to play with. Everyone fighting for the top bunk.

Confession: she is jealous of her students

Not because they can
drink all night without bodily damage
or dark shadows. Not because of how fucking
cute they look with their sweaters on
inside out, caps on backwards.
Not because life is one big, beautiful
pick-up opportunity and with each
ending, they suffer exquisite torture,
can't come to class, for the pain. Or even
because they're too young to understand
it's not grand agonies but mechanical details
that get you, in the end: like not being able
to find the high beams, after he left.
But because they make poems with no
effort at all, fingers wild on keys
adding this, taking away that, slipping here
instead of there and ta da: *there is a lawyer of dust over everything,*
one of them wrote without even knowing, a metaphor
I'd steal for. And I have. So send the lawyers of dust
after me. They'll find me. Here. Caught in the low beams.

Bergamot

Ten tipsy
well-bred women
in mauve satin
gowns snapping mauve
bath towels at each other
in a tree house,
      long green bottles
      below,
          empty.

Loosestrife

It's hard to hate loosestrife, anything loose,
saucy, not dour. There's a witch-hunt, all right:
It's a foreigner, must be burned,
one book claims. Multiculturalism
doesn't extend to botany. Flowers
with purple spiked hair.

Driving this country – long, river-bound
swaths of Quebec or prairie mourning
its lost elevators – loosestrife gives us
the cheerful, purple finger from its
love-ins in ditches. Ministry of Wild Things
says: *out of control, no family values at all.*

Have you ever been called floozy but
you're basically good? Do you ask only for
a little fun before frost, a romp in the grass
(well yes, couple of things
you shouldn't have done but otherwise
it's straight up)? Is your bad reputation

undeserved? Then you see what I mean.

Blue jay lesson

All about scam. No good if it's easy right
side up. All about kicking bird butt
in a great-looking blue tux. Feed the blue jay
inside you:
                       didn't you want to
throttle a finch today
send some up-
start into the sky
with no supper
iron the ruffles
off the grouse?
Yes, you did
                out there
in your stocking hat, flinging sun-
flower seeds from the deck
                   feeding an ancient
outlaw habit.

The sign on my door

Had I applied myself,
I could have stolen.
          – Karen Solie, "Thief"

I've written in this room with withered larkspur
in ice bucket for how long? Two, three, days? Enough time
to grow fruit flies. The culprit: a badly freckled banana
I planned to eat on first looking into the blank
screen's blinding white light. It's a sad sliver of moon
now, snuffed at both ends. When did it stop
being fruit? The larkspur's stalk leans like a dull green
fishing pole (held by ghost) hung with seventeen
mauve and white gazebos. Lonely gazebos. I'm never
all I can be. *Had I applied myself,*

I wouldn't need to share space with spoilage.
I wouldn't feel compelled to place positive spins on things.
I wouldn't have to strand my sense of humour in compromising
locales, sing *Good Night, Irene* alone in the shower. Had things
turned out not like this, I'd cross out "do not," leave only
"disturb" on the sign on my door. I'd declare it open season
on anything. Talk signifiers, talk Britney Spears, burn my wick,
disquiet my imaginary quiet, talk anything but regret.
I did the time warp, now I have to pay. I can never
be all I am. If you know what's good for you, don't knock, no
matter which way the sign's turned.
Leave me grieve the hours *I could have stolen.*

The hours

"Mrs. Dalloway said she would buy the flowers herself."
                     – Virginia Woolf

said she would   said she would   she would

buy the flowers

             the flowers

                        flowers herself her

selves:

             Clarissa, Laura, Virginia.

What's in a day? Did you see the way her shoe drifted from her
foot, lace tangled in seaweed's
dark scrim? Did you catch the unremitting creak and scuzz
of the ancient lift she took to his loft? Were you convinced
the warrior having returned, deserved perfection on his birthday,
not some lousy, lopsided cake? Have you howled
in one way or another or

another to be *heard*? Do you agree it might have been avoided
simply by moving back to town? Surely you've felt the jolt
of the capital yourself? Have you ever said oh, let's have *buckets*
of roses? Have you fled flood water rising in your own hotel room
in the middle of a

special day? Would you rip the drapes from your windows on the
last day of your life, would you
want *that* much light   would you

savage the party that way: *her* party   flowers

the flowers   the selves

Abacus abalone abandon

Ninth grade. Miss Redpath read *In Flanders Fields*. I wept.
"It's only a poem," she said, "it's ok." It wasn't,
she marred me. After that, I went nowhere
without "We are the dead. Short days ago
we lived" throbbing between my earmuffs.
Mr. Green, grade ten. Bone class. Naked numbers
wintered on the board. Not one
leaf remained, my teeth chattered for them, knees
following suit, knock, knock (*Numeric fallacy*,
Redpath might have declared – despite her
starched heart, she had a lathe mind, could turn
the old phrases!). No pathetic vibrating allowed
in Green's room – he sent me down to Detention,
they said "write out the dictionary." Before abattoir,
they said "come back, you're missing too much" (in that
windowless foyer, I learned abacus, abalone, abandon!).
Eleven: eyes on muscle-braided legs, sprinter girl
ahead (left in dust, I longed to return
to A). Knew, rounding the final curve, I'd suffer
a stroke, down the road. A massive
teenage epiphany hit my heaving chest – one day
I wouldn't breathe at all!
Bonjour, twelve – repeat after Madame Bleu:
"Bonjour, Monsieur Tibot. Bonjour, Madame Tibot.
Have you met my wife?" Sad, sad people, the Tibots.
No one cried for their question-answer life. No one failed
save moi. (Vice-principal White trapezed "something very amiss"
across my report. Rocket science, Whitey! – poppies blow though
only in poems, words bloom in dank hallways where photo-
synthesis can't possibly occur which doesn't begin to address

the lovely, chestnut-haired racer who soon
will only run ruined in the aching
tilted track in my very-amiss head). Year thirteen, I splashed
a magenta mountain across a page. Pranced a row of pearled
trees along its craggy, main artery. It was winter, it was
called *Abacus Abalone Abandon, The End.*
"Honey, those are the prettiest purple alps I ever
laid eyes on!" – Mrs. Palette – at last
something that sang, a note that couldn't be curtailed, detained,
tallied to the nth nothing. That wouldn't be left breathless.

Acknowledgements

I am grateful to the Canada Council for the Arts for supporting the writing of these poems.

Heartfelt thanks to my editor, Barry Dempster, for his diligence, sensitivity, and sparkling ear. On the champagne rack of editors, Barry is Dom Perignon.

Various events and individuals fostered this collection: The Sage Hill Writing Experience; The Banff Writing Studio; The Sarah Lawrence College Summer Seminar for Writers; The Silence and Conversation Symposium at St. Peter's College, Saskatchewan; George Sanderson; Gertrude Sanderson; Don McKay; Anne Simpson; Tim Lilburn; Thomas Lux; Fred Wah; Katie Lynes; Christian Riegel; Anthony Chan; Andrew Stubbs; Dave Margoshes, Rob McLennan. Thanks to all.

I am indebted to Glenn Priestley for cover art and design work, and to K. Priestley for design work.

"Dead people's clothes" is for Ian and Laura Cull. "*The Guess Who* Play North Bay – One Night Only" is for Laurie Kruk. "Shooting the little bear" is for Tim Quick. "Career Day at Diefenbaker High" is for Judith Kalman. "Bergamot" is for Don McKay. "Blue jay lesson" is for Christian Riegel. "*The Hours*" is for Sina Queyras. "Water lilies" is for Karen Lochhead. "Abacus abalone abandon" is dedicated to the memory of Mrs. L. Stanley, my high-school art teacher. "Brave" is for my mother.

"Abacus abalone abandon" received the 2001 Bliss Carman Poetry Award. "On rereading Flannery O'Connor's 'Good Country People'" placed second in the 2000 Bliss Carman Poetry Award competition. "Brave" was awarded first prize in *Contemporary Verse 2*'s "Shades of Colour, Shades of Light" contest in 1999. "What we learned on the highway near St. John's" placed second in the "Confederation 50" contest sponsored by *TickleAce* in 2000. "Summer house, Southampton, 1939" received first prize in Brucedale Press' spring poetry contest in 1999.